THIS NOTEBOOK BELONGS TO:

IF LOST, RETURN TO OWNER VIA :

Printed in Great Britain
by Amazon

35838053R00070